Primordial Variable Method Kettlebell Training:

Become a Special Force

By Steven Helmicki

ISBN 978-0-557-28623-2

A full set of kettlebells is required to perform this training as it is exactly laid out. Pairs of 4kg, 6kg, 8kg, 12kg, 16kg, 24kg, 32kg, 40kg, 48kg. The exercises are always performed light to heavy.

This methodology develops enormous explosive power endurance. It also allows field soldiers to maintain a high level of quickness during prolonged absence from formal gym access.

Record all workouts in the Primordial Workout Log.

After all eight workouts are performed in one month taking 3 days between sessions, the trainee begins with workout 1 and adding one additional round to each complex and training every other day. Straight set numbers remain a constant. 100 reps remains 100 reps throughout training. This is repeated twice and then the trainee returns to completing the program in its original format and escalating the training again in the exact method stated above with the exception of greater velocity on the movements.

The interactive based re-calculation of training is purposely left to the devices of the purchaser of this manual. Intimacy with your training is vital to your long term success. Own your physical destiny by economy of training and a relaxed demeanor.

Workout 1

Kettlebell swings 4kg x 1 immediately followed by 6kg x 1 immediately followed by 8kg x 1 repeat sequence 8 times non-stop

Hydration

Kettlebell bent rows deadstop 4kg x 2 immediately followed by 6kkg x 2 immediately followed by 8kg x 2 repeat 10 times non-stop

Hydration

Kettlebell high pulls 4kg x 2 immediately followed by 6kg x 2 immediately followed by 8kg x 2 repeat 6 times non-stop

Hydration

Kettlebell curls 4kg x 2 immediately followed by 6kg x 2 immediaely followed by 8kg x 2 repeat 6 times non-stop

Hydration

Kettlebell triceps extensions 4kg x 2 immediately followed by 6kg x 2 immediately followed by 8kg x 2 repeat 6 times non-stop

Workout 2

Kettlebell Front Squats 12kg x 2 immediately followed 16kg x 2 repeat 6 times non-stop

Hydration

Ketlebell sumo deadlifts 12kgs x 2 immediately followed by 24kgs x 2 repeat 6 times non-stop

Hydration

Kettlebell overhead press 12kg x 2 immediately followed by 16kg x 2 repeat 6 times non-stop

Hydration

Kettlebell swings 12kg x 2 immediately followed by 16kg x 2 repeat 6 times non-stop

Workout 3

Kettlebell pullovers 4kg x 4 immediately followed by 6kg x 4 immediately followed by 8kg x 4 repeat 5 times non-stop

Hydration

Double kettlebell swings 4kg x 2 immediately followed by 6kg x 2 immediately followed by 8kg x 2 repeat 10 times non-stop

Workout 4

Kettlebell clean and jerks 8kg x 2 immediately followed by 16kg x 2 repeat 4 times non-stop

Hydration

Kettlebell snatches 8kg x 2 immediately followed by 16kg x 2 repeat 4 times non-stop

Hydration

Kettlebell front squats 8kg x 3 immediately followed by 16kg x 3 repeat 4 times non-stop

Hydration

Kettlebell side bends 16kg x 3 immediately followed by 32kg x 3 repeat 3 times non-stop

Hydration

Kettlebell swings 8kg x 1 immediately followed by 16kg x 1 repeat 4 times non-stop

Workout 5

Kettlebell sumo deadlifts 24kg x 2 immediately followed by 48kg x 2 repeat 4 times non-stop

Hydration

Kettlebell shrugs 24kg x 2 immediately followed by 48kg x 2

Repeat 6 times non-stop

Hydration

Kettlebell swings 24kg x 3 immediately followed by 48kg x 3 repeat 4 times non-stop

Hydration

Kettlebells side bends 24kg x 3 immediately followed by 48kg x 3 repeat 4 times non-stop

Workout 6

Kettlebell sumo deadlift 4kg x 2 immediately followed by 8kg x 2 immediately followed by 16kg x 2 immediately followed by 32kg x 2 immediately followed by 48kg x 2 repeat 3 times non-stop

Hydration

Kettlebell bent rows 4kg x 1 immediately followed by 8kg x 1 immediately followed by 16kg x 1 immediately followed by 32kg x 1 immediately followed by 48kg x 1 repeat 3 times non-stop

Hydration

Kettlebell shrugs 4kg x 4 immediately followed by 8kg x 4 immediately followed by 16kg x 4 immediately followed 32kg x 4 immediately followed by 48kg x 4 repeat 3 times non-stop

Hydration

Kettlebell swings 4kg x 1 immediately followed by 8kg x 1 immediately followed by 16kg x 1 immediately followed by 32kg x 1 immediately followed by 48kg x 1 repeat 3 times non-stop

Workout 7

Kettlebell front squats 4kg x 5 immediately followed by 8kg x 5 immediately followed by 12kg x 5 repeat 3 times non-stop

Hydration

Kettlebell high pulls 4kg x 5 immediately followed by 8kg x 5 immediately followed by 12kg x 5 repeat 3 times non-stop

Hydration

Kettlebell bent over laterals 4kg x 5 immediately followed by 8kg x 5 immediately followed by 12 kg x 5 repeat 3 times non-stop

Hydration

Kettlebell curls 4kg x 5 immediately followed by 8kg x 5 immediately followed by 12kg x 5 repeat 3 times non-stop

Hydration

Kettlebell swings 4kg x 5 immediately followed by 8kg x 5 immediately followed by 12kg x 5 repeat 3 times non-stop

Workout 8

4kg flush

100 front squats

100 stiff-legged deadlifts

100 overhead presses

100 bent over rows

100 curls

100 triceps exensions

Reformat Workout 1:

Reformat Workout 2:

Reformat Workout 3:

Reformat workout 4:

Reformat Workout 5:

Reformat Workout 6:

Reformat Workout 7:

Flush remains the same.

Add Additional rounds to workout 1:

Add additional rounds to workout 2:

Add additional rounds to workout 3:

Add additional rounds to workout 4:

Add additional rounds to workout 5:

Add additional rounds to workout 7:

Flush remains the same.

Go back to original programming Complete the entire manual again at much improved velocity. The speed of the movement is absolutely vital to training effectiveness.

Remain Strong always in your midst danger remains.

Explosive quickness and the elasticity created from variable method kettlebell training can be transferred to human contact power in devastating fashion.

Endure complete mental clarity by focusing on controlling your breath, form and velocity. You will grow quickly in all areas of life.

Be without ego but remain mentally strong. Serve God and Justice.

Stop racism and live peace.

Reach out to a brother or sister in need and give unconditionally from your love.

Always remain a warrior, courage and honor until death.

www.ingramcontent.com/pod-product-compliance
Ingram Content Group UK Ltd.
Pitfield, Milton Keynes, MK11 3LW, UK
UKHW041902190726
13854UKWH00003B/1031